Norwegian Recipes
Old-time Favorites

Collected by Norma Wangsness
Rosemaling by Norma Wangsness

Revised and expanded

Edited by Ann M. Bauer, Dorothy Crum, Michelle Nagle Spencer, M
Joan Liffring-Zug Bourret, Liz Rolfsmeier, and Maureen Patt

About the Author

Norma Wangsness, volunteer for Vesterheim, the Norwegian-American Museum, preserves her Norwegian-American heritage in many ways. She paints in the Telemark style and won the coveted gold medal at Vesterheim's rosemaling competition in 2000. She also paints ornaments, which are shown on the inside and back cover of this book, in addition to being a great cook. In compiling this collection, Norma selected family favorites and recipes she has used for years. Norwegian-American cooks are noted for their use of almond and dill for delicate and flavorful seasonings. These recipes also include the old favorites of delicious cookies, light cakes, sweet breads, lefse, and the traditional root vegetables.

ISBN 1-932043-04-7   Copyright 2002 Penfield Books   www.penfieldbooks.com

Chapters

Approximate Metric Equivalents

1/4 teaspoon = 1.23 milliliters
1/2 teaspoon = 2.46 milliliters
3/4 teaspoon = 3.7 milliliters
1 teaspoon = 4.93 milliliters
1-1/4 teaspoons = 6.16 milliliters
1-1/2 teaspoons = 7.39 milliliters
1-3/4 teaspoons = 8.63 milliliters
2 teaspoons = 9.86 milliliters
1 tablespoon = 14.79 milliliters
2 tablespoons = 29.57 milliliters
1/4 cup = 59.15 milliliters

1/2 cup = 118.3 milliliters
1 cup = 236.59 milliliters
2 cups or 1 pint = 473.18 milliliters
3 cups = 709.77 milliliters
4 cups or 1 quart = 946.36 milliliters
4 quarts or 1 gallon = 3.785 liters

Temperature
To get Celsius (Centigrade) when Fahrenheit is known: subtract 32, multiply by 5, divide by 9.

Sites of Norwegian-American Interest

Vesterheim (Vesterheim means western home)
The Norwegian-American Museum
Decorah, Iowa
This is one of the great folk art museums of North America devoted to a single immigrant culture. Nordic Fest is held the last full weekend in July in Decorah, about one hundred fifty miles south of Minneapolis-St. Paul, Minnesota.

Little Norway
Blue Mounds, Wisconsin
The beautiful collection at Little Norway includes antiques, an ornate reproduc-

continued

tion of a 12th-century stavkirke (Norwegian timbered church), and other fascinating buildings, including a stabbur and a house with a sod roof. Open spring through fall, Little Norway is twenty-five miles west of Madison, Wisconsin.

The Chapel in the Hills
Rapid City, South Dakota
This stave church duplicates one built more than eight hundred years ago in Borgund, Norway. Carved dragon heads are on the roof. There is also an imported Norwegian stabbur (a building used for food storage).

The Nordic Heritage Museum
Seattle, Washington
This facility is devoted to the people from the five Scandinavian countries: Sweden, Norway, Finland, Denmark, and Iceland.

The Heritage-Hjemkomst Center
Moorhead, Minnesota
The center features a 20th-century Viking ship and exhibits that tell the story of the Red River Valley.

'I Jesu Navn'
Norwegian Table Prayer

I Jesu Navn går vi til bords,
Spise og drikke på ditt ord.
Deg Gud til aere, oss til gavn
Så får vi mat i Jesu navn.

In Jesus' name we take our place,
To eat and drink upon Thy grace.
To Thy honor and our gain
We take our food in Jesus' name.

Beverages

Glogg

1 bottle red port
12 figs
1/2 cup candied ginger
1 stick cinnamon
1/2 cup raisins

1/2 cup hazelnuts
1/2 cup slivered almonds
2 tablespoons dried
       orange peel (optional)
1 cup cubed sugar

Soak all but sugar overnight in the port. Before serving, bring to a slow boil and pour over sugar. Serve warm. If a stronger drink is desired, add 1/2 pint vodka or brandy. Serves about 15 with one refill.

Fruit Juice Glogg
Gløgg

2 cups apple juice
1 cup grape juice
2 tablespoons sugar
1 stick cinnamon

4 cloves
1 orange peel, pared from orange
1/3 cup slivered almonds
1/3 cup raisins

Combine juices, sugar, spices, and orange peel in a saucepan. Bring to a boil. Remove cloves, cinnamon stick, and orange peel. Place several almonds and raisins in punch cups and pour hot punch over them. Serve immediately.

Norwegian Eggcream
Eggedosis

10 egg yolks

1/2 cup sugar

1 cup brandy

Nutmeg

Beat egg yolks and sugar together until thick and creamy. Gradually beat in brandy. Sprinkle with nutmeg. Makes 1 quart.

Soups and Salads

Split Pea Soup
Ertesuppe

1 cup split peas
1 small ham hock
2 quarts water

2 medium-sized carrots
1/2 small onion, finely chopped
Salt to taste

Wash peas and soak overnight in enough water to cover. In the morning, boil the ham hock in water for 1/2 hour. Add the peas and soaking water to the ham hock kettle; cover and boil slowly until the peas are mushy, about 1 hour. Remove the ham hock. Scrape and slice carrots and add, with onion, to cooked peas. Salt if necessary. Cook for another 30 minutes. If there is meat on the ham hock, remove, finely chop, and return to soup. Serves 6.

Spinach Soup
Spinatsuppe

2 pounds fresh spinach, chopped
2 quarts chicken stock
3 tablespoons butter
2 tablespoons flour

1 teaspoon salt
1/4 teaspoon white pepper
Dash of nutmeg
3 hard-cooked eggs, sliced

Add spinach to boiling stock; simmer 8 to 10 minutes. Remove; strain spinach. Set aside. Melt butter in saucepan; whisk in flour, salt, pepper, and nutmeg; gradually add 1 to 2 cups stock, stirring until well blended. Add flour mixture to hot stock, stirring with a wire whisk; simmer over low heat 5 minutes. Add spinach and continue to simmer, uncovered, 5 minutes. Serve with egg slices on top. Makes 4 to 6 servings.

Yellow Pea Soup
Gul Ertesuppe

2 cups dried yellow peas
7 cups cold water
2 pounds boneless pork shoulder
3 leeks, sliced
2 medium carrots, scraped and shredded
2 medium onions, chopped

2 teaspoons chopped parsley
1 teaspoon crushed marjoram
1/2 teaspoon crushed thyme
1/4 teaspoon ground ginger
1 teaspoon salt
Spicy brown mustard (optional)

Wash peas. Heat to boiling in water; boil a few minutes. Remove from heat. Soak 30 minutes. Add pork shoulder and rest of ingredients, except mustard. When water boils, reduce heat; simmer partially covered 1-1/2 hours, until pork and peas are tender. Remove pork. Cut into thin slices; serve with mustard.

Cauliflower Soup
Blomkålsuppe

2 tablespoons vegetable oil
1/2 cup chopped onion
1 small carrot, peeled and grated
1 cup chopped celery
1 medium-sized head cauliflower, cut
    into flowerets
2 tablespoons chopped parsley
8 cups chicken stock

"bouquet garni" (1/2 teaspoon
    peppercorns, 1 teaspoon tarragon,
    1/2 bay leaf)
1/4 cup butter
1/4 cup flour
2 cups milk
1 cup half-and-half
Salt to taste
1 cup sour cream

Heat oil in a large stockpot over medium heat. Sauté onion until tender. Add carrot and celery and sauté lightly. Add cauliflower and 1 tablespoon parsley. Reduce heat, cover, and cook for about 15 minutes; stir occasionally. Add chicken stock and bouquet garni and bring to a boil; reduce heat and simmer for about 5 minutes. To thicken, melt butter in a saucepan; stir in flour and slowly add milk, stirring constantly until thick. Remove from heat and stir in half-and-half. Stir sauce into simmering soup. Season to taste with salt and simmer 15 to 20 minutes. Before serving, remove bouquet garni; mix about 1/2 cup hot soup with sour cream. Stir sour cream mixture into soup; add remaining parsley and reheat. Makes 10 to 12 servings.

Tomato Soup
Tomatsuppe

4 medium-sized tomatoes
Pinch of baking soda
2 cups whole milk

Salt and pepper to taste
Butter to taste
Spekekjött (dried beef)

Wash, peel, and slice tomatoes. Place in a medium-sized saucepan and cook over medium heat until very soft. Remove from heat. Add pinch of soda to tomatoes to prevent curdling. In another pan, bring milk to a boil and remove from heat. Force the cooked tomatoes through a strainer and add to the milk. Season to taste with salt, pepper, and butter. Serve with Spekekjött.

Cucumber Soup
Agurksuppe

1/2 medium-sized onion, chopped
1 medium-sized carrot, sliced
4 cups chopped celery with leaves
1 tablespoon butter
3 medium-sized cucumbers, peeled
    and diced
1/4 teaspoon thyme

1/2 teaspoon tarragon
6 cups chicken broth
2 eggs
1 cup cream
1/8 teaspoon lemon juice
Sweet paprika to taste
Sesame seed to taste

Sauté onion, carrot, and celery in butter until almost tender. Add cucumber,

continued

thyme, tarragon, and chicken broth; cook, covered, until vegetables are soft. Purée and return to low heat. Beat eggs with cream and lemon juice. Gradually add about 1 cup of the hot soup to this mixture. Add egg mixture slowly to soup, stirring constantly until well-blended and creamy. Season to taste. Before serving, sprinkle with sweet paprika and sesame seed.

Cheese Soup
Ostesuppe

2 cups chopped celery
1/2 large green pepper, chopped
2 cans cream of mushroom soup
Milk equal to 2 cans soup
1/2 cup tomato purée
1/4 teaspoon ground coriander

1/2 teaspoon white pepper
2 cups shredded Cheddar cheese
1/4 cup sour cream
1/2 cup dry sherry (optional)
2 tablespoons chopped parsley

Cook celery and green pepper in boiling water until tender. Drain. Mix soup and milk, then mix with celery and pepper. Heat in double boiler over hot (not boiling) water. Stir in tomato purée, coriander, white pepper, cheese, and sour cream. Stir until smooth and hot. Add sherry just before serving. Garnish with parsley.

Fish Soup
Fiskesuppe

2 tablespoons butter or margarine
4 medium-sized potatoes, diced
2 leeks or scallions, sliced
1 stalk celery, diced
2 teaspoons salt
1 teaspoon pepper

5 cups water
1 pound fresh or frozen fish fillets, cut into 1-inch pieces
1 tablespoon chopped fresh dill or 1 teaspoon dried dill

Melt butter in large heavy stockpot; sauté potatoes, leeks, and celery until glazed. Add salt, pepper, and water. Boil for 10 minutes, until vegetables are almost tender. Add fish; boil 10 to 15 minutes more. Sprinkle with dill just before serving. Serves 4.

Ale Stew
Ølsuppe

1-1/2 pounds lean beef, cut into thin slices (round steak is good)
3 tablespoons margarine or butter
3 medium-sized onions, sliced

8 medium-sized potatoes, scrubbed and sliced
1 teaspoon salt
1/8 teaspoon pepper
1 pint light ale

Brown beef slices in 2 tablespoons margarine; remove from pan and set aside. Keep warm. Sauté onions in remaining margarine until lightly browned. In a heavy saucepan, place alternate layers of meat, onions, and potatoes; sprinkle with salt and pepper. Pour pan drippings over layers. Add ale, cover, and simmer gently until meat and potatoes are tender, about 1-1/2 hours. Makes 4 to 5 servings.

Trondheim Soup
Trondhjemssuppe

1/2 cup barley or rice
2 quarts water
1/2 pound dried, pitted prunes
1/2 cup raisins
4 tablespoons fresh lemon juice
3 tablespoons sugar

1/2 cup red fruit juice (cherry or cranberry)
1/2 cup whipping cream
1/4 teaspoon salt
2 beaten egg yolks

Cook barley in boiling water 1 hour. Add prunes and raisins; simmer until tender, 1/2 hour. Combine lemon juice, sugar, fruit juice, whipping cream, salt, and egg yolks. Beat with a wire whisk; add 1 cup of hot soup stock. Add to soup and whisk until hot. Serve hot or cold.

Norwegian Fruit Soup
Søtsuppe

1/3 to 3/4 cup quick-cooking tapioca
2 quarts water
1 can prunes, pitted
1/2 cup light and dark raisins
1 cup dried apricots
2 sticks cinnamon, broken

1/2 teaspoon salt
Juice of 1 lemon
1 can pitted dark Bing cherries, with juice
1 cup sugar
1 pint grape juice
1 pint red wine

Soak tapioca overnight in water. Add prunes, raisins, dried apricots, cinnamon sticks, and salt. Bring to a boil. Reduce heat, cover, and simmer until tapioca is clear, stirring occasionally. Add remaining ingredients. When soup boils, remove from heat. Serve hot or cold.

Norwegian Vegetable Salad
Grønnsaksalat

1 cup finely shredded cabbage
2 carrots, peeled and grated
2 cooked beets, coarsely grated

1 apple, peeled, cored, and grated
1 tablespoon lemon juice

Combine vegetables and grated apple; mix in lemon juice. Toss with dressing for coleslaw (page 33). Serves 6.

Red Bean and Celery Salad

Salat med Røde Bønner og Selleri

2 (15-ounce) cans red kidney beans
2 cups sliced celery, with leaves
6 scallions, finely sliced
1/2 medium-sized green pepper,
    coarsely chopped
1 cup chopped sweet pickle

Dressing
1/2 cup olive oil
1/2 cup red wine vinegar
2 teaspoons dill seed
1 teaspoon tarragon powder
1/2 teaspoon ground cardamom
1 teaspoon curry powder
1 teaspoon salt

Drain and rinse beans in cold water. Combine with celery, scallions, pepper, and pickle. Blend all dressing ingredients and pour over bean mixture. Marinate for at least 1/2 day.

Aquavit Herring
Sild i Aquavit

4 fillets of salt herring

2/3 lemon, peeled and thinly sliced

1-1/3 teaspoons crushed juniper
    berries

3/4 medium-sized onion, thinly sliced

1/3 tart apple, peeled, cored, and cut
    into large julienne strips

3 tablespoons Aquavit

Marinade

5 tablespoons vinegar

1/4 cup water

1/4 cup sugar

4 whole cloves

1 slice lemon peel (1 x 2 inches)

1/2 teaspoon caraway seeds

1/2 teaspoon aniseed

1/4 teaspoon ground allspice

1/2 teaspoon cracked black peppercorns

Soak herring in cold water overnight. Rinse and dry. Combine marinade ingredients in a saucepan and bring to a boil. Remove from heat and cool. Cut herring into 1-inch pieces and layer with lemon slices, juniper berries, onion, and apple in a large glass jar or bowl. Add Aquavit to marinade and strain into layers. Cover tightly and marinate herring in refrigerator 1 to 2 days before serving. Can be refrigerated 1 week.

24-Hour Salad

2 eggs, beaten
4 tablespoons sugar
4 tablespoons vinegar
2 tablespoons butter
2 cups mini-marshmallows

1 cup cream, whipped
2 cups white cherries or grapes
2 cups pineapple chunks, drained
2 oranges, sectioned, or 1 small can
mandarin oranges, drained

Combine eggs, sugar, vinegar, and butter. Cook in double boiler. Stir constantly until a thick custard is formed. Cook, then add remaining ingredients. Pour into a pretty crystal bowl and chill 24 hours.

Dressing for Coleslaw
Dressing til Kålsalat

1 cup white vinegar
1 teaspoon celery seed
1 cup salad oil
1 cup sugar

1 teaspoon dry mustard
1 teaspoon salt
1 medium-sized onion, grated

Heat (but do not boil) vinegar and celery seed. Set aside to cool. Combine and beat salad oil, sugar, dry mustard, salt, and onion. Combine the two mixtures and beat well. Shake well before using. Dressing may be kept refrigerated 3 to 4 weeks.

Breads
and Sandwiches

Norwegian Rye Bread
Rugbrød

2 packages dry yeast
2 cups lukewarm water, divided
4-1/2 cups white flour, divided
1 teaspoon white sugar
1-1/2 cups rye flour
2/3 cup firmly packed brown sugar
3-1/2 tablespoons dark, unsulphured
   molasses

3 tablespoons butter, melted
1 tablespoon finely grated orange peel
1 teaspoon salt
1 teaspoon vinegar
Pinch of aniseed
Vegetable shortening

continued

Soften yeast in 1 cup warm water. Combine 1 cup white flour and white sugar in a large bowl. Add yeast mixture; let stand 5 minutes. Stir in remaining water. Add remaining white flour and all other ingredients except shortening. Stir until combined. Turn onto floured surface and knead until dough is smooth and satiny, adding additional white flour if necessary. Place dough in large bowl greased with shortening; turn dough to grease all surfaces. Cover with cloth and let rise until doubled, 1 hour. Punch down and return to floured surface; knead until no longer sticky. Return to bowl and coat top lightly with shortening. Cover and let rise until doubled, 30 minutes. Divide dough in half and form into 2 eight-inch round loaves. Place on greased baking sheets; cover and let rise until doubled, 30 minutes. Bake in preheated 350° oven until lightly browned, 25 to 30 minutes.

Oatmeal Flatbread
Havremel Flatbrød

1/2 cup sugar
3/4 cup melted butter
1/2 teaspoon salt
1 teaspoon soda

1-1/2 cups buttermilk
3 cups white flour (or 2 cups white
    and 1 cup whole-wheat)
2 cups quick-cooking oats

Cream together sugar and melted butter. Add salt. Add soda to buttermilk; add the creamed mixture alternately with flour. Add the oats. Divide mixture into 2 log shapes. Divide each into 1/3-cup portions and shape into a round ball. Press down and roll on pastry cloth with a rolling pin covered with a pastry sleeve. Roll

continued

paper-thin. Use a lefse stick, or roll on rolling pin. Lift and unroll on cookie sheet. Either cut with a pastry cutter into squares before baking or bake and then break into pieces. Bake at 350° until lightly browned, 8 minutes. Remove, cool, and stack. Store in covered container.

Butter Horn Rolls
Smørhorn

1 cake yeast
1/2 cup sugar, divided
1 cup lukewarm milk
1/2 cup butter

Salt to taste
3 eggs
4 cups flour

Crumble yeast and mix with 1 tablespoon sugar. Combine and add milk, remaining sugar, butter, and salt. Add beaten eggs. Mix in flour to make soft dough. Let rise until doubled. Punch down; divide into halves, rolling each into a round. Cut each round into 16 pie-shaped pieces. Shape butter horn by rolling toward small end. Put in lightly greased pan to rise (until not quite doubled). Bake at 350° until flaky, 20 minutes. While warm, top with butter. Makes 32 rolls.

Hardtack

2 cups white flour
2 cups graham flour
1/2 cup white sugar
1 teaspoon soda

1/2 teaspoon salt
1 tablespoon aniseed
1/2 cup shortening
1-1/2 cups buttermilk

Mix dry ingredients. Cut in shortening. Add buttermilk. Mix until a soft dough is formed. Roll out thin on a floured board. Cut into diamond-shaped pieces. Place on a greased cookie sheet. Bake at 400° for 12 to 15 minutes.

Dill Casserole Bread
Brød med Dill

1 package yeast
1/4 cup warm water
1 cup creamed cottage cheese
2 tablespoons sugar
1 tablespoon instant minced onion
1 tablespoon butter

2 teaspoons dill seed
1 teaspoon salt
1/4 teaspoon baking soda
1 egg
2 to 2-1/4 cups flour

Dissolve yeast in water. Heat cottage cheese to lukewarm. Combine sugar, onion, butter, dill, salt, soda, and egg with cottage cheese/yeast mixture. Add flour to form stiff dough. Cover; let rise until doubled. Punch down. Turn into well-greased 1-1/2-quart casserole or 8-inch round pan. Let rise 30 to 40 minutes or until light. Bake 40 to 50 minutes at 350°. Brush with butter; sprinkle with salt.

Beer Bread
Vørterkake

2 tablespoons yeast
1-1/4 cups warm milk
5 to 6 cups unbleached flour, divided
1/2 cup sugar
1 tablespoon salt

1/2 teaspoon ground cloves
1/2 teaspoon pepper
1-1/2 cups beer
1/2 cup light corn syrup
2 cups rye flour
1 cup raisins

Dissolve yeast in milk. After 5 minutes, add 1 cup unbleached flour, sugar, salt, cloves, and pepper. Cover; let stand 40 minutes, until light and bubbly. Add beer, syrup, rye flour, raisins, and enough unbleached flour to make dough stiff. Knead 10 minutes on floured breadboard. Let rise 1 hour. Divide and place in 3 greased loaf pans. Let rise 10 to 15 minutes. Cover with foil. Bake 40 minutes at 350°.

Rusk

Kavring

1/2 cup margarine
1/3 cup sugar
1 cup white flour
1 cup whole-wheat or rye flour

1 teaspoon soda
2 teaspoons baking powder
1/2 teaspoon cream of tartar
3/4 cup buttermilk

Cream together margarine and sugar. Sift together other dry ingredients. Add to creamed mixture alternately with buttermilk. Roll flat with rolling pin to 1/4-inch thickness on floured pastry board. Cut 2-inch rounds. Place on ungreased baking sheet and bake at 400° for 10 to 15 minutes or until lightly browned. **To serve:** Split each biscuit in half. Bake at 200° on a baking sheet 5 minutes or until lightly browned. Makes four dozen. May freeze.

Lefse

This basic recipe was developed by the late Ida Sacquitne, a recognized expert on making lefse, and is in the book Notably Norwegian. *Note: Sugar is often omitted in Norway.*

5 well-packed cups riced potatoes
1/2 cup margarine
3 Tbsp. powdered sugar

2 cups flour
1 tsp. salt

Boil, then rice potatoes through a potato ricer. Add margarine while potatoes are still warm. Cool to room temperature. Add powdered sugar, flour, and salt. Mix with your hands. Knead well and then roll into a log. Cut and measure into 1/3-cup portions and make round ball of each portion. Pressing it down by hand will make it easier to keep round while rolling out. Dust the large canvas-like cloth lefse "board" with flour. Press dough down, turn over, and press down again.

With pastry sleeve-covered rolling pin, roll as thin as possible into large 14-inch circles to fit lefse grill. (The secret of making thin lefse is using a covered rolling pin. For an even thinner dough, use a grooved lefse rolling pin for the last roll across the dough.) Roll dough on a lefse stick. Bake on lefse grill or griddle. Bake a minute or two, until bubbles and brown spots appear, then turn with lefse stick. Fold each lefse into halves or quarters. Cool between cloths and store in plastic bags. Makes 18. Spread with butter or sprinkle with brown or white sugar. Roll up to eat. **Note:** Lefse may be made without official lefse utensils and cloths, but follow the principles of method provided by these traditional tools.

Strawberry Nut Bread
Jordbærkake med Nøtter

1/2 cup butter
3/4 cup sugar
1/2 teaspoon vanilla
1/8 teaspoon lemon extract
2 eggs
1/2 cup strawberry jam

1/2 cup sour cream
1-1/2 cups flour
1/2 teaspoon salt
1/4 teaspoon soda
1/3 teaspoon cream of tartar
1/4 cup chopped walnuts

Cream butter, sugar, vanilla, and lemon extract until light. Add eggs, one at a time, beating well after each. Combine strawberry jam and sour cream and add alternately with dry ingredients to creamed mixture. Add walnuts. Bake in greased loaf pan 50 minutes at 350°. Cool 10 minutes before removing from pan.

Oatmeal-Date Bread
Havrekake med Dadler

1 cup boiling water
1 cup quick-rolled oats
2 eggs, beaten
1/2 cup white sugar
1 cup brown sugar
1/2 cup shortening
1/2 cup chopped dates

1/2 cup chopped nuts
1 cup flour
1/2 teaspoon cinnamon
1 teaspoon baking soda
1/2 teaspoon cloves
1 teaspoon salt

Combine boiling water and oats; let stand until cool. Mix eggs, sugars, shortening, dates, and nuts. Sift dry ingredients together and stir into date-nut mixture. Add oatmeal. Bake in greased loaf pan 1 hour at 350°.

Christmas Bread
Julekake

2 cups milk, scalded
1 to 2 cakes yeast
1/4 cup warm water
1 cup and 1 tablespoon sugar, divided
7 to 8 cups flour, divided
1/2 cup butter

1 cup raisins
1 cup chopped citron
2 teaspoons cardamom
1/2 cup blanched almonds
2 teaspoons salt
2 eggs

Cool milk to lukewarm. Dissolve yeast in water and 1 tablespoon sugar. To the milk, add 1 cup sugar, yeast mixture, and half the flour. Beat well. Add butter, fruit, cardamom, almonds, salt, eggs, and remaining flour to make stiff dough. Knead, cover, and let rise until doubled. Punch down and form 2 loaves. Let rise. When doubled, bake 1 hour at 350°.

Waffles
Vafler

4 eggs, separated
2 cups milk
3 cups sifted flour
5 teaspoons baking powder

1 teaspoon salt
2 teaspoons sugar
2/3 cup melted butter or margarine

Beat egg yolks; add milk, sifted dry ingredients, and melted butter. Beat egg whites and fold into yolk mixture. Pour into greased, hot waffle iron. Cook until edges are lightly browned.

Poppy Seed Bread
Valmuefrøkake

3 eggs
2-1/4 cups sugar
3 cups flour
1-1/2 cups oil
1-1/2 cups milk
4 tablespoons poppy seeds (less if
   preferred)
1-1/2 teaspoons almond extract

1-1/2 teaspoons butter extract
1-1/2 teaspoons baking powder
1 teaspoon salt

Topping
1/2 teaspoon each: vanilla, butter, and
   almond extract
1/4 cup orange juice concentrate
3/4 cup powdered sugar

Cream eggs and sugar; add remaining ingredients. Mix well; divide. Pour into 3 small, greased, floured loaf pans. Bake 1 hour at 350°; spread on topping.

Apple Coffee Cake
Eplekake

1 package yeast

1/2 cup warm water

4-1/3 cups flour, divided

1 teaspoon salt

2 cups and 6 tablespoons sugar, divided

1 cup and 1 stick margarine or butter, divided

1 egg

1 cup milk

3 cups sliced apples

Cinnamon

Mix yeast and water; set aside. With fingers or pastry blender work 4 cups flour, salt, 6 tablespoons sugar, and 1 cup margarine until small particles form. Add egg, milk, and yeast mixture. Let stand overnight. In the morning, divide dough and

continued

press out on 2 large cookie sheets. Pare and slice apples and layer on top of each coffee cake. Sprinkle cinnamon liberally over apples. Combine 1 stick margarine with 2 cups sugar and 1/3 cup flour. Mix with pastry blender and spread over coffee cake. Bake at 350° for 15 to 20 minutes.

Mother's Doughnuts
Mors Smultringer

2 eggs, beaten
1 teaspoon vanilla
1 cup sugar
3 tablespoons melted shortening
1 cup milk

1/2 teaspoon salt
1 teaspoon almond extract
1 teaspoon nutmeg
2-1/2 teaspoons baking powder
3-1/4 to 3-3/4 cups flour

Mix all ingredients in order; spoon onto floured board. Toss lightly to coat with only enough flour to make a soft dough: just firm enough to handle, not sticky. Flatten; cut with well-floured double cutter or two sizes of biscuit cutter. Gather scraps; repeat. Heat oil to 350° and maintain medium temperature. Fry doughnuts until browned, turning once. Drain.

Potato Pancakes
Potetpannekaker

These are good with pork sausages.

2 cups grated raw potatoes
1/4 cup milk
2 eggs, slightly beaten

1 teaspoon salt
1 teaspoon baking powder
1/4 cup flour

As potatoes are grated, add milk at once to prevent discoloring. Add remaining ingredients. Drop by spoonfuls on hot greased skillet and fry to golden brown on both sides. Reduce heat after browning and cook until potatoes are done.

Sandwich Suggestions

Both open-faced and "filled" sandwiches are typical light Norwegian fare. The following is a compilation of some of our favorite sandwich combinations:

1. Smoked salmon with European scrambled eggs
2. Liver paté with beets and olives
3. Sliced pork roast with cold sweet-sour cabbage (surkål)
4. Crab meat with capers, mayonnaise, chives, cucumber, and lemon wedges
5. Russian salad, radish, and cucumber
6. Roquefort on dark bread with ripe olives and radishes
7. Meatball with sweet pickle, pimiento, olive, and parsley

continued

8. Pork with sweet mustard, cucumber, and green pepper
9. Egg salad with curry, sweet pickle, and parsley
10. Cream cheese and pineapple
11. Finely chopped pecans and seedless raisins blended with mayonnaise
12. Mashed bananas, peanut butter, and mayonnaise
13. Sardines and chopped hard-cooked eggs, moistened with lemon juice and Worcestershire sauce
14. Crab meat and minced celery, mixed with salad dressing
15. Ground leftover pot roast with celery and pickles, moistened with mayonnaise
16. Caviar on lettuce with sliced hard-cooked or scrambled eggs

Liver Paté
Leverpostei

1 pound calf liver, cut into
   1-inch chunks
1-1/4 pounds pork fat, 1/2 pound cut
   into 1-inch chunks
1/2 cup chopped onion
4 anchovy fillets, chopped
2 tablespoons butter
2 tablespoons flour
1 cup heavy cream
3/4 cup milk

3 eggs
1 teaspoon salt
1/2 teaspoon white pepper
1/2 teaspoon ground allspice
1/2 teaspoon crushed marjoram
1/4 teaspoon ground ginger
1/4 pound fresh mushrooms,
   chopped
1/4 cup dry white wine

continued

Finely grind liver and 1/2 pound pork with onions and anchovies. **To prepare white sauce:** Melt butter; stir in flour until blended. Whisk in cream and milk; cook over low heat until smooth and thick. Stir 1/2 cup of white sauce into ground liver mixture. Mix in remaining ingredients except rest of pork fat. Cut remaining pork fat lengthwise into 1/8-inch-wide strips. Arrange overlapping strips to cover bottom and sides of a 9 x 5-inch loaf pan, or comparable mold. Reserve enough strips to cover top of paté. Shape liver mixture into prepared pan and cover top with pork fat strips. Cover and place in pan of water and bake at 350° until knife inserted in center comes out clean, about 2 hours. Remove baking pan from water and cool to room temperature before refrigerating. Chill thoroughly. Remove from loaf pan, cut in thin slices, and serve.

Salmon Sandwiches
Laksesmørbrød

1/2 pound fresh cooked salmon, flaked,
   or 1 (7-3/4-ounce) can salmon
1-1/2 cups shredded Swiss cheese
1/2 cup mayonnaise
1/2 cup finely chopped celery

1/4 cup chopped ripe olives
3 scallions, chopped
1 teaspoon Worcestershire sauce
1 medium-sized loaf French bread
Softened butter

Combine all ingredients except bread and butter. Slice bread loaf in half, lengthwise. Spread both halves with softened butter and salmon mixture. Place under broiler and heat just before serving, 5 minutes. Cut individual pieces, open-faced, to serve.

Pressed Sandwich Meat
Rullepølse

2-1/2 pounds beef flank
4 teaspoons salt
1 tablespoon pepper
2 teaspoons ginger
1/2 teaspoon sugar

1 pound beef round, thinly sliced
1/2 pound pork tenderloin, sliced
1/4 pound beef, finely ground
1/4 pound pork, finely ground
3 tablespoons minced onion

Trim all fat from flank. Flatten with meat pounder. Mix salt, pepper, ginger, and sugar, and rub flank with part of mixture. Place sliced beef and pork on half of flank. Combine ground beef and ground pork with remaining seasonings and minced onion. Spread over beef and pork slices. Roll meat tightly; tie together with strong string and secure in piece of cheesecloth. Put in heavy kettle and cover with water. Simmer 2-1/2 to 3 hours, until tender. Remove from kettle. Place roll between two heavy plates under heavy weight to press out moisture. Keep in a cool place several hours or overnight. Remove cloth and string. Refrigerate. Cut in thin slices; serve cold. Makes 10 to 12 servings.

Meat and Seafood

Spareribs

4 pounds pork spareribs
1/2 cup chopped onion
2 tablespoons vegetable oil
1 cup catsup
1/4 cup vinegar
2 tablespoons Worcestershire sauce

1-1/2 to 2 tablespoons sugar
1 teaspoon pepper
2 teaspoons chili powder
1/4 teaspoon paprika
1 teaspoon salt
1 cup water

Cut spareribs into 3 or 4 portions. Bake, uncovered, at 450° for 20 minutes. Brown onions in oil, then add remaining ingredients. Simmer slowly for 20 minutes. Pour sauce over partially baked ribs and continue baking at 350° for 1-1/2 hours. Baste frequently.

Mock Beef Stroganoff

1 pound hamburger
1/2 cup chopped onion
1 teaspoon salt
1 teaspoon seasoned salt
1 teaspoon Worcestershire sauce
Dash of celery salt, garlic, and sage

1/4 cup catsup
1/4 cup flour
1-1/3 cups buttermilk
6 ounces of noodles
1 can French onion rings

Brown hamburger and onion; add remaining ingredients, except noodles and onion rings. Cook and drain noodles. Add to hamburger mixture. Bake 20 minutes at 350°. Sprinkle onion rings over top. Return to oven and bake for another 10 minutes.

Meatballs
Kjøttboller

2 quarts water
1 medium-sized onion, chopped
Few stalks celery, finely chopped
Mixture of ground pork, beef, and veal
    (preferably unseasoned)
1 cup cream
1 egg

1 tablespoon cornstarch
Salt and pepper to taste

Gravy
2 cans consommé
3 tablespoons flour
1 can cream of mushroom soup

Bring water, onion, and celery to a boil in a deep kettle. Mix ground meat, cream, egg, cornstarch, and seasonings; form balls. Drop meatballs into boiling liquid;

continued

reduce heat and simmer until they are firm. Remove from broth and put meatballs into a greased baking dish. Mix consommé, flour, and mushroom soup; pour over meatballs. Bake at 350°, covered, for 1 hour. Uncover and bake 1/2 hour more until well-browned. This can be prepared and frozen before baking.

Royal Pot Roast
Slottsstek

2 tablespoons butter
2 tablespoons vegetable oil
4 pounds boneless beef (round, rump, or chuck)
1 cup finely chopped onion
3 tablespoons flour
1 tablespoon dark corn syrup
2 tablespoons white vinegar

2 cups beef stock
1 large bay leaf
6 anchovy fillets, washed and drained
1 teaspoon whole peppercorns, crushed and tied in cheesecloth
Salt to taste
Black pepper, freshly ground, to taste

In heavy 5- to 6-quart ovenproof pan or casserole, melt butter and oil over mod-

continued

erate heat. Brown meat on all sides. Remove meat from pan. Add onion to meat juices in pan and cook over moderately high heat 6 to 8 minutes, stirring occasionally until lightly browned. Remove from heat. Add flour. Stir gently to blend. Add dark syrup, vinegar, and stock. Add bay leaf, anchovies, and bag of peppercorns. Return meat to pan; cover and bring to a boil. Preheat oven to 350°. Place pan on shelf in lower third of oven, regulating heat so liquid barely simmers. Meat should be tender in about 3 hours. Transfer roast to heated platter. Cover to keep warm. Skim fat from meat juices; discard bay leaf and peppercorns. Add salt and pepper to taste. If more flavor is needed, boil briskly, uncovered, over high heat to concentrate. Serve gravy with the meat.

Fried Calf's Liver

2 pounds calf's liver	Pepper to taste
1 pint water	1 egg, beaten
1/4 cup vinegar	Cracker crumbs (or flour)
1 teaspoon salt	2 tablespoons butter

Soak liver in water and vinegar at least 2 hours. Remove membrane and cut liver into thin slices. Pat dry; salt and pepper; dip into beaten egg, then into cracker crumbs or flour. Fry in browned butter over medium heat until well-done. Makes 4 to 6 servings.

Veal with Sour Cream
Kalvekjøtt i Rømme

1/4 cup finely chopped onion
3 tablespoons butter, divided
3 tablespoons vegetable oil, divided
4 slices of veal, 3/8 inch thick and
pounded to 1/4 inch thick
1 cup sour cream
1/2 cup shredded Gjetöst (goat cheese)
Salt and pepper to taste

Sauté onions in 1 tablespoon butter and 1 tablespoon oil in large skillet over low heat until transparent. Remove onions; set aside. Add remaining butter and oil; sauté veal slices until lightly browned. Remove to platter; keep warm. Reserve thin layer of fat in pan. Return onions; cook for a few minutes over high heat until slightly brown. Reduce heat; slowly add sour cream and cheese, stirring until smooth. Do not boil. Season. Return veal to skillet; simmer 1 to 2 minutes.

Veal Fricassee
Kalvefrikassé

2 pounds veal
Water to cover veal
2 teaspoons salt
1 tablespoon butter

1/2 cup flour
2 medium-sized carrots, sliced and cooked
Parsley, chopped

Cut meat in many places. Cover in boiling water; add salt. Boil slowly until bones come off easily. Remove meat when tender; skim fat from broth. Drain and reserve broth. Melt butter; stir in flour until blended. Add enough broth to make gravy; cook to desired thickness. Cut meat into slices or small pieces and place on serving dish; top with carrots. Cover with gravy and sprinkle with parsley.

Veal Loaf
Kalvekjøttbrød

3 pounds ground veal
3/4 pound ground salt pork
1 cup crushed crackers
2 eggs, beaten

1 cup boiling water
1 teaspoon sugar
4 teaspoons salt
2 teaspoons pepper

Combine veal and salt pork until well-blended. Add remaining ingredients; mix thoroughly. Shape into a greased loaf pan and bake at 300° for 2 hours.

Liver Loaf

2 pounds ground liver
1/2 pound chopped side pork
2 teaspoons salt
1/2 teaspoon pepper
1/4 teaspoon nutmeg

1/4 teaspoon ground cloves
2 eggs, beaten
3/4 cup milk
Onion, chopped (as desired)
1 cup flour

Preheat oven to 400°. Combine all ingredients and put into greased loaf pan. Place in preheated oven and reduce heat to 300°; bake for 1 hour. Serve warm or chilled.

Blood Sausage
Blodpølse

1/2 cup uncooked rice or 1 cup pearl
  barley
2 quarts pork or beef blood (pork is
  preferred)
1/2 cup sugar
Dash of ground cloves
1/2 teaspoon ground ginger

1/2 teaspoon ground allspice
1 tablespoon salt
3 to 4 cups flour
Cloth bags (4 x 10 inches)
3/4 cup raisins (optional)
1-1/2 pounds suet or fresh pork, diced

Cook rice or barley in boiling salted water until nearly done. Drain and combine
with blood and seasonings. Add enough flour to make a thin batter, just a little

thicker than pancake batter. Wet cloth bags. Pour batter into bags, adding raisins (if desired) and suet or pork at intervals so it is distributed throughout. Fill bags about 3/4 full to allow for expansion of the sausage. Sew or tie ends of bags tightly and place in slightly salted boiling water. Simmer 1-1/2 to 2 hours or until well-done. When ready to serve, remove from bags and slice.

Serving suggestions: While hot, top with butter and syrup. Slice cold and fry in pork drippings or butter until brown; cover with sour cream and simmer 5 to 10 minutes.

Christmas Ham
Juleskinke

1 fresh ham (9 to 10 pounds)
1 cup sugar, divided
3 tablespoons fine salt
4 tablespoons saltpeter, divided

2 bottles light beer
2 bottles dark beer
3 cups coarse salt

Rub ham with 1 tablespoon sugar, fine salt, and 3 tablespoons saltpeter. Leave 24 hours. Boil beer, coarse salt, and remaining sugar and saltpeter together. Cool and pour over ham. Leave in brine 3 weeks, turning daily. Hang to dry in an airy place. Smoke following smoker directions. When smoked, simmer 4 hours in unsalted water. Cool in stock. Remove rind. Serve hot or cold. Store in stock to keep ham juicy.

Ham Loaf

2 pounds ground pork
1 pound ground cured ham
1 egg, beaten
1 cup bread crumbs
1/2 cup milk
3 tablespoons tomato soup
1/2 teaspoon paprika
1/4 teaspoon salt

1 medium-sized onion, sliced

Mustard Sauce
1/2 cup tomato soup
1/2 cup sugar
1/2 cup mustard
1/2 cup vinegar
3 egg yolks, beaten

Mix all ham loaf ingredients, except onion, and shape in a loaf pan. Top with onion. Bake 1-1/2 hours at 350°. Serve with sauce. **To make sauce:** Combine sauce ingredients; cook in double boiler, stirring until thick.

Glazed Ham Balls
Glaserte Skinkeboller

1/2 pound ground ham
3/4 pound ground pork
2/3 cup rolled oats (uncooked)
1 egg, beaten
1/2 cup milk
1/3 cup brown sugar

2 tablespoons flour
1 teaspoon dry mustard
2/3 cup fruit juice (pineapple, apricot, or peach)
2 tablespoons vinegar
6 whole cloves

Thoroughly mix ham, pork, rolled oats, egg, and milk; chill. Place, ball-shaped, in shallow baking pan. Bake 1 hour at 300°. Drain fat. Combine remaining ingredients in saucepan; cook until thick. Pour over balls and bake 15 minutes. Serve in center of baked noodle or rice ring. Garnish with parsley and carrot petals.

Lamb and Cabbage
Fårikål

3 to 4 pounds lamb, trimmed of fat
   and cut into 1-1/2-inch cubes
3 tablespoons butter or margarine
1/2 cup flour
Pepper to taste

1 large onion, sliced
2 pounds white cabbage, coarsely
   sliced
2 tablespoons salt (approximately)
3 cups chicken broth

Brown lamb cubes in butter over medium heat a few at a time until evenly browned. Remove from pan and place in a large bowl. Sprinkle meat with flour and toss until well-coated; use all the flour. Pepper to taste. In 6-quart ovenproof

continued

casserole, layer lamb cubes, onion slices, and cabbage slices, using half the ingredients each time. Salt each layer lightly. End with a layer of cabbage. Pour fat from pan used to brown the meat. Pour chicken broth into pan and boil, scraping any browned meat particles from bottom of pan into the broth. Pour broth over layered meat, onion slices, and cabbage slices. Bake at 350° for 1-1/2 hours or until meat is tender. Serves 6.

Note: This dish can be made ahead of time and reheated. Boiled potatoes and parsley go well with this dish.

Lamb Roast
Lammestek

1 tablespoon salt
1 tablespoon freshly ground pepper
1 (5-pound) leg of lamb
3 onions, sliced
3 carrots, sliced

1 cup hot beef broth
1-1/2 cups hot, strong coffee
1/2 cup heavy cream
1 tablespoon sugar

Preheat oven to 450°. Rub salt and pepper into lamb and place on rack in roasting pan. Surround lamb with onions and carrots. Roast 30 minutes; skim fat. Reduce oven to 350°; add broth, coffee, cream, and sugar. Basting frequently, continue roasting 40 minutes to 1 hour, to desired doneness. Transfer lamb to a warm platter. Force gravy through a sieve or purée.

Roast Venison
Dyrestek

3 to 4 pounds haunch of venison,
    deboned
Salt to taste
Freshly ground pepper to taste
1 teaspoon chopped parsley
Pinch of dried thyme
3 tablespoons butter, softened

1-1/2 cups beef stock or bouillon
1 tablespoon butter
1 tablespoon flour
1 cup whipping cream
2 teaspoons red currant jelly
1/2 ounce Gjetöst (goat cheese)

Rub meat with salt, pepper, parsley, and thyme and spread with softened butter.
Tie cord, if needed, to hold shape. Place on rack in shallow roasting pan and sear

in preheated 475° oven for 20 minutes. When meat is browned, reduce heat to 375° and add beef stock to pan juices. Roast, uncovered, for 1-1/4 hours; baste with juices frequently. When roast reaches desired doneness, remove to large platter; cover to keep warm. Skim fat from pan juices. Measure remaining juices and reduce or add water to make 1 cup. In a saucepan, melt butter, stir in flour, and cook over low heat until flour is browned, but not burned. Whisk the pan juices into flour mixture until smooth; add whipping cream, jelly, and cheese. Whisk until jelly and cheese are incorporated into a smooth sauce. Do not boil. Heat only until sauce is hot. Serve separately with sliced venison.

Roast Goose

Stekt Gås

1 (9- to 10-pound) goose
Salt to taste
2 pounds tart apples, peeled, cored, and chopped
1 pound prunes, pitted, halved, soaked
Flour
6 tablespoons butter, melted in 1 cup hot water

Wash goose thoroughly; pat dry. Salt inside and out. Prick with sharp-tined fork (every second square inch). Stuff cavity with apple/prune mixture. Place breast-side up on rack in large open broasting pan. Roast 45 minutes at 450°. Remove from oven; drain drippings. Sprinkle with a little more salt; dust with flour. Reduce oven to 350° and bake, 20 minutes per pound. When flour browns, baste often with water/butter mixture. Sprinkle lightly with flour after each basting.

Lobster

Hummer

Lobster tails [1 (8-ounce) tail per serving]
1 large onion, minced
2 medium-sized carrots, shredded
1/4 pound butter
1/4 cup brandy
1 teaspoon fennel

1 teaspoon salt
1/8 teaspoon cayenne pepper
1/8 teaspoon saffron
1/2 teaspoon lemon juice
2 cups heavy cream

Prepare lobster, but cook no more than 10 minutes after liquid boils. When done, remove and rinse in cold water. Slice meat into 1-inch pieces; set aside. Sauté onion and carrots in butter until tender. Add lobster; sauté until lobster is glazed (not brown). Heat brandy; pour over lobster and set aflame; stir until flame dies.

Blend in remaining ingredients. Stir until thick. Serve over hot rice.

Baked Fish
Bakt Fisk

3 pounds baking fish (bass, halibut, or other firm fish)
Salt and pepper to taste
Oregano to taste
1/2 cup olive oil
3 firm tomatoes, sliced
3 green onions, chopped
3/4 to 1 cup chopped parsley
1 clove garlic
15 to 20 Saltines, crushed
Butter
2 large onions, sliced into rings
Lemon slices for decorating
1 cup water

Put fish in greased dish; sprinkle with salt, pepper, oregano, and oil. Add tomato, green onion, parsley, and garlic. Top with cracker crumbs; dot with butter. Add onion rings, lemon, and water; bake 45 minutes at 350°. Serves 6.

Baked Trout
Bakt Ørret

1 (4- to 5-pound) fresh trout
1 teaspoon salt
4 cups coarse bread crumbs
1/2 cup melted fat (bacon, sausage, or
    chicken)

Sage to taste
Pinch of thyme
Pinch of chervil

Clean trout, wipe dry, and sprinkle with salt, inside and out. **To make stuffing:** Mix remaining ingredients. Stuff fish and secure. Place on rack in a baking pan and bake at 375°; allow 10 to 15 minutes per pound. Baste with pan juices. Serve with melted butter and lemon or a savory sauce.

Creamed Crab
Stuet Krabbe

1 cup crab meat
2 tablespoons flour
2 tablespoons butter
1 cup cream
3 tablespoons sherry

Buttered crumbs
1 egg, beaten
Paprika to taste
Salt to taste
Cayenne to taste

Flake the crab meat, removing all bones carefully. Make a white sauce of the flour, butter, and cream; add crab and sherry. Fill the buttered crab shells or small ramekins. Top with buttered crumbs and glaze with egg. Sprinkle paprika, salt, and cayenne over top and brown in a hot oven.

Codfish

Klippfisk

1 pound salt codfish
2 tablespoons butter
2 tablespoons flour
1/4 teaspoon salt

1 teaspoon curry powder
Paprika to taste
1 cup milk
Onion juice to taste

Soak codfish in cold water 2 hours to freshen. Melt butter; add flour mixed with salt, curry, and paprika. Blend well; add milk gradually, stirring until very smooth. Bring to a boil; boil 2 minutes. Add onion juice to taste. Drain cod, rinse, and boil in unsalted water 10 minutes. Serve with sauce.

Boiled Salmon
Kokt Laks

4 to 6 pounds salmon, dressed
3 quarts water
1/4 cup lemon juice
3 tablespoons salt
Parsley and lemon for garnish

Sauce
1/2 cup sour cream
1/4 teaspoon salt
1/4 teaspoon sugar
1/2 teaspoon horseradish

Put salmon on big cheesecloth. Tie ends of cloth. Bring water, lemon juice, and salt to boil in large pot with bottom rack. Rest salmon on rack. Cover. Simmer 10 to 12 minutes or until flaky. Remove from pot and put on platter. **Sauce:** Mix sauce ingredients. When ready to serve, remove cheesecloth from salmon; scrape off skin. Garnish with parsley and lemon and serve with sauce.

Salmon Pie
Laksepai

2 tablespoons butter
1/4 cup flour
2 cups milk
1/4 teaspoon butter flavoring
1 (1-pound) can salmon or tuna

2 cups cooked peas
1/4 cup chopped pimiento
1 tablespoon minced onion
Biscuits

Melt butter; stir in flour until smooth. Add milk, stirring constantly until thick. Add butter flavoring. Gently fold in salmon, peas, pimiento, and onion. Pour into greased 2-quart casserole. Make round biscuits; place on top of casserole. Bake 12 to 15 minutes at 350°.

Salmon Soufflé
Laksesufflé

1 cup milk
1 cup soft bread crumbs
1 tablespoon butter
1/2 teaspoon salt

3 eggs, separated
1-1/2 cups drained, flaked salmon
1 teaspoon lemon juice

Scald milk. Add bread crumbs, butter, and salt. Add slightly beaten egg yolks and cool mixture to lukewarm. Beat egg whites until stiff but not dry. Add salmon and lemon juice to milk-yolk mixture. Fold in beaten egg whites. Spoon into lightly oiled casserole. Place in pan of hot water and bake at 375° for 45 minutes.

Oyster Soufflé
Østers-Sufflé

10 oysters
3 tablespoons butter
3 tablespoons flour

Salt and pepper to taste
1/2 cup cream
2 eggs, separated

Shell oysters and rinse; remove broken shells. Put in saucepan; cover with water. Simmer until edges curl and oysters are plump. Drain; cut each into 2 to 4 pieces. Melt butter. Add flour and seasoning; blend until smooth. Add cream; stir until smooth. Boil, stirring, 5 minutes. Remove from heat; cool. Add beaten yolks, oyster pieces, and stiffly beaten egg whites. Bake in buttered individual casseroles or 1 baking dish 20 minutes at 375°.

Fish Mousse
Fiskemousse

1 pound halibut or other tender fish
3 egg whites
1 cup heavy cream or evaporated milk
1 teaspoon salt

1/2 teaspoon pepper
Cayenne, nutmeg, celery salt, or a few
   drops onion juice to taste

Finely chop fish. Put in bowl in ice water. With a wire whisk, beat in egg whites until frothy. Stir in cream or evaporated milk slowly. Salt, pepper, and season to taste. Stir well; let stand 1 hour. Pour into 1-1/2-quart mold or small timbale molds. Set in pan of water, 1 inch deep. Cover. Bake 45 minutes or until firm at 350°. May also cook on stovetop on low heat, with water barely simmering. Turn onto platter; serve with sauce.

Shrimp and Cheese Casserole

6 slices bread, toasted and cubed
1 pound prepared shrimp
1/2 pound English cheese, grated
1/4 cup margarine

1/2 teaspoon dry mustard
3 eggs, beaten
1 pint milk

Make in layers. Let stand at least 3 hours or overnight. Bake, covered, for 1 hour at 350°.

Macaroni and Salmon Loaf

1/2 (7-ounce) package macaroni, cooked
2 eggs, separated
1 cup milk
1 can salmon

2 cups bread crumbs
1 tablespoon butter
1 tablespoon salt
Creamed peas

Cook macaroni according to box directions. Beat egg whites to stiff peaks. Mix all ingredients, folding in whites last. Bake in a casserole, placed in a pan of water, at 350° for 1 hour. Serve creamed peas over loaf.

Vegetables and Side Dishes

Roe Potato Cakes
Rogn og Potetkaker

1 large fresh roe
5 potatoes, boiled and mashed
1 teaspoon flour
1 teaspoon potato flour

1 teaspoon salt
1/2 teaspoon pepper
1/2 teaspoon ginger
Butter or margarine for frying

Prick roe and remove the membrane. Mash roe and stir into the finely mashed potatoes. Add the flour and potato flour, salt, pepper, and ginger; blend thoroughly. Form the potato-roe mixture into small round flattened cakes and fry them in butter or margarine until golden brown. Makes 4 to 6 servings.

Wild Rice

1 cup wild rice
1-1/2 teaspoons salt
1 tablespoon vinegar

1 packet dried onion
3 cups rich chicken stock

Wash rice thoroughly. Cover with boiling water; let stand 20 minutes. Drain. Place in casserole with tight cover. Mix salt, vinegar, and dried onion with the chicken stock and add to rice. Cover. Bake 1-1/2 hours at 300°. Serves about 6, more if there are additions such as water chestnuts, green pepper, or sliced almonds. For a complete supper dish, add chicken and mushrooms.

Basic Noodles

2 egg yolks
1 teaspoon softened lard
2 tablespoons cream

1/4 teaspoon salt
1/4 teaspoon baking powder
Sifted flour

Beat egg yolks. Add lard, cream, salt, and baking powder. Mix well, and add enough sifted flour to make a soft dough that will roll out thin without being sticky. Turn onto a floured work space and roll very thin or to desired thickness. Cut wide strips, then stack and cut noodles to desired width. These may be cooked immediately or dried and stored for later use. Sift flour over cut noodles before using. Noodles should be frozen if stored for a long time.

Norwegian Potato Balls
Potetballer

8 anchovy slices, finely chopped
1 tablespoon flour
1 tablespoon chopped parsley
1/2 teaspoon salt
1/2 teaspoon dry mustard
1/4 teaspoon pepper

1/8 teaspoon mace
6 medium-sized potatoes, peeled,
   cooked, and mashed
1 egg yolk, beaten
1 cup dry bread crumbs
Vegetable oil for deep-frying

Add minced anchovies, flour, parsley, and seasonings to mashed potatoes. Shape into balls, about 1 tablespoon each. Dip potato balls into egg yolk and coat with bread crumbs. Fry a few at a time in deep fat until golden brown. Drain on absorbent paper.

Perfect Boiled Potatoes

Boiled potatoes are very popular in Norway and are served with almost every dinner. A typical Norwegian food, they are homegrown root vegetables that can be kept through the long, cold, dark winter months.

Traditional Norwegian cooks boil unpeeled potatoes, beginning with cold water, and after boiling peel and soak them in cold water for an hour. Then they recook the potatoes in salt water. When they are heated thoroughly, they are drained and returned to the pan until dry. Potatoes are kept under a cloth to absorb any excess water before serving.

Party Potatoes

8 to 10 medium-sized potatoes
1 (8-ounce) package cream cheese
1 cup sour cream
Chives to taste

Garlic salt to taste
Butter to taste
Paprika to taste

Peel potatoes and cook until tender; drain. Mash potatoes. Beat softened cheese and sour cream until well-blended. Add to hot potatoes, beating until light and fluffy. If too stiff, thin with milk. Add chives and garlic salt to taste. Turn into a 2-quart casserole; dab with butter and sprinkle with paprika. Brown at 350° for 30 minutes. Can be made the day before, refrigerated, and heated before serving.

Escalloped Potatoes

1 quart peeled, thinly sliced potatoes
1-1/2 teaspoons salt
1/8 teaspoon pepper
2 tablespoons flour

2 tablespoons grated onion
2 tablespoons butter
2 cups hot milk

Place half the potatoes in greased shallow 2-quart baking dish. Sprinkle with half the salt, pepper, flour, onion, and bits of butter. Repeat and add milk. Cover and bake at 350° for 1-1/2 hours. Remove cover for last 20 minutes to brown, if desired.

Orange-Glazed Sweet Potatoes

2 pounds sweet potatoes
2/3 cup sugar
1 tablespoon cornstarch
1 teaspoon salt

1/2 teaspoon orange peel, grated
1 cup orange juice
2 tablespoons butter or margarine

Heat oven to 400°. Pare sweet potatoes; cut each in half lengthwise and place in a 1-1/2-quart casserole. In small saucepan, mix sugar, cornstarch, salt, and orange peel. Stir in orange juice and butter and cook until thick. Pour over the sweet potatoes and bake, covered, 1 hour, basting occasionally.

Sweet-Sour Cabbage
Surkål

This recipe is good served with roast pork.

1 head cabbage
1 teaspoon salt
2 tablespoons sugar

1/4 cup vinegar
2 tablespoons caraway seeds

Shred cabbage very fine. Add other ingredients. Cover with water and simmer for 2 to 3 hours.

Red Cabbage
Surkål

1 large head red cabbage
2 tablespoons butter, divided
1-1/4 teaspoons caraway seeds
1 tablespoon flour

1 teaspoon salt, divided (more to taste)
2 cups meat stock or water
1 tablespoon vinegar
1 tablespoon sugar

Remove core of cabbage and soak in cold salt water 10 minutes. Drain. Shred into fine strips. Grease kettle with 1 tablespoon butter; layer alternately cabbage, caraway seeds, and dots of butter. Sprinkle each layer with flour and salt. Pour stock over. (You should barely see cabbage.) Cover. Simmer 1-1/2 hours, stirring frequently. Do not boil dry; add water if needed. Stir in vinegar, sugar, and salt.

Glazed Carrots
Glaserte Gulerøtter

6 medium-sized carrots
2 cups boiling water
1 teaspoon salt

4 tablespoons butter
2 teaspoons sugar
1 tablespoon finely chopped parsley

Scrape and trim carrots; cut each into 4 pieces. Place in saucepan; pour boiling water over; add salt, butter, and sugar. Cover with lid. Let boil gently until carrots are tender and water is almost evaporated. Shake pan so carrots are turned and glazed. Sprinkle with chopped parsley. Serves 6.

Baked Celery
Bakt Selleri

1 large bunch celery, trimmed
Water to cover
1 medium-sized onion or 1 bunch
   scallions, minced
1 medium-sized green pepper, chopped
2 tablespoons butter

3 ounces cream cheese
3 ounces gjetöst cheese
1-1/2 cups cream
3 tablespoons dry sherry (optional)
Salt and pepper to taste

Cut celery into 1-inch pieces; include some leaves. Cook in water, until almost tender. Drain; reserve liquid. Sauté onion and green pepper in butter until soft. Blend 1-1/2 cups reserved liquid, cheeses, cream, and sherry. Pour into lightly oiled baking dish. Bake 15 minutes at 400°, until thick. Salt and pepper to taste.

Sautéed Cucumbers
Stekt Agurk

3 medium-sized cucumbers
6 tablespoons flour
1-1/2 teaspoons salt
1/2 teaspoon pepper

1 teaspoon crushed dill
2 tablespoons butter
1/4 teaspoon fenugreek

Pare and slice (1/4 inch thick) cucumbers. Mix flour, salt, pepper, and dill; dredge cucumber slices in this mixture. Melt butter; add fenugreek. Sauté cucumber slices quickly until golden brown and crisp.

Pickled Beets
Stekt Agurk

1/2 cup white vinegar

1/2 cup sugar

1 (1-pound) can sliced beets with juice, separated

1/2 to 1 teaspoon salt

Pepper to taste

Whole cloves

In stainless steel or enameled 1-1/2- to 2-quart saucepan, mix vinegar, sugar, beet juice, salt, pepper, and a few whole cloves tied in a cloth bag. Bring to a boil and boil briskly 2 minutes. Put beets in a deep glass, stainless steel, or enamel bowl. Pour hot marinade over beets and cool, uncovered. When mixture is room temperature, cover bowl with tightly fitting cover. Refrigerate at least 12 hours.

Beet Mold
Rødbetsalat i Form

1 package lemon gelatin
1 cup cold water
3/4 cup beet juice from canned beets
1/4 cup vinegar or lemon juice

2 cups chopped beets
2 tablespoons prepared horseradish
1/2 teaspoon salt

Dissolve gelatin in cold water; add beet juice and vinegar or lemon juice. Stir in beets, horseradish, and salt. Pour into ring mold, prerinsed in cold water. Chill until firm. Fill center with salad dressing to serve.

Cookies, Cakes, and Desserts

Berliner Kranser

3 hard-cooked egg yolks
1 cup sugar
4 raw egg yolks

5 cups flour
1 pound butter
4 egg whites, beaten

Mash hard-cooked yolks; add sugar gradually and raw yolks one at a time, mixing thoroughly. Mix flour and butter until particles are finely blended. Add yolk mixture by forcing through sieve. Work by hand until a pliable dough forms. Roll small pieces of dough by hand to pencil thickness, 5 inches long; lap over ends. Layer in pans with waxed paper; chill. When ready to bake, dip each cookie into foamy egg white; sprinkle with sugar. Bake at 350° until golden brown, 8 minutes. Makes 100 cookies. Store in an air-tight container in cool place.

Eggless Lace Cookies
Flarn uten Egg

1/2 cup flour

1/2 cup sugar

1/4 teaspoon baking powder

1/2 cup oats

1/3 cup butter, melted

2 tablespoons heavy cream

2 tablespoons light corn syrup

1 tablespoon vanilla

Stir together flour, sugar, and baking powder; add rest of ingredients and stir well. Drop by teaspoons about 4 inches apart onto a lightly oiled cookie sheet. Bake at 375° until lightly browned, 4 to 6 minutes. Let stand a minute before removing to rack to cool.

Spritz

1 cup powdered sugar
1 cup butter
2 egg yolks, or 1 egg
1 teaspoon vanilla

2 cups flour
1/2 teaspoon cream of tartar
1/2 teaspoon soda
Pinch of salt

Sift and tap sugar to measure 1 cup. Cream sugar and butter; add egg yolks and vanilla; mix well. Sift dry ingredients and blend into creamed mixture. Place dough in cookie press, using star tip. Shape dough into circles to form wreaths or "S" shapes. Make a test cookie; if it does not hold its shape, add a bit more flour. Bake at 350° for 6 to 9 minutes or until lightly browned.

Sand Bakkels

1/2 cup butter	1 teaspoon vanilla
1/2 cup shortening	1/4 teaspoon almond extract
3/4 cup sugar	2-1/4 cups flour
1 egg	

Cream butter and shortening with sugar; add egg and flavorings and beat well. Sift flour and gradually add to creamed mixture. Mix well. Turn dough onto waxed paper and wrap. Chill 45 minutes. Preheat oven to 350°. Cut thin slices of dough and press into sand bakkel tins, starting at the bottom and working up. Bake on cookie sheet 15 minutes or until golden brown. Cool in tins, then turn out. (May also roll out dough and bake on regular cookie tins.)

Date Pinwheel Cookies
Daddelrull

Cookies
1 cup brown sugar
1 cup white sugar
1 cup margarine
1 tablespoon milk
2 eggs
1 teaspoon vanilla
4 cups flour

1 teaspoon soda
1 teaspoon salt

Filling
1/4 cup sugar
1/4 cup water
1/4 cup finely chopped nuts
1 package pitted dates

Cookies: Cream sugars and margarine. Mix in milk, eggs, and vanilla. Add dry ingredients to form a firm dough. On a floured surface, roll dough to 1/4 inch thick.

Filling: Combine all filling ingredients and spread on dough.

Roll up and chill several hours. Slice and bake at 350° until golden brown, about 8 minutes.

Spiced Hermits

1 cup shortening
2 cups sugar
3 eggs
1 teaspoon cinnamon
1 teaspoon nutmeg
1/2 teaspoon cloves

2 teaspoons lemon extract
1 teaspoon soda dissolved in 1 tablespoon hot water
2 cups raisins, rinsed and ground
3-1/2 cups all-purpose flour

Combine ingredients in order given and chill dough. Roll out thinly and cut with large round cookie cutter. Sprinkle with sugar and bake at 350° for 10 to 12 minutes. Makes a large batch.

Rosettes

2 eggs
1 teaspoon sugar
1/4 teaspoon salt
5 drops vanilla

1 cup milk
1 cup flour
Shortening for deep-frying
Powdered sugar

Beat eggs, sugar, salt, vanilla, milk, and flour until batter is smooth. Too much beating makes rosettes blistered and tough. Have hot shortening ready in deep kettle. Leave rosette iron in hot shortening several minutes. The iron must be hot before dipping into batter. Wipe excess fat from iron and dip hot iron in batter, being careful that batter does not come above edge of form. Quickly immerse in

continued

hot shortening. Fry 20 seconds or until color desired.

Jolt rosette off iron and repeat. Place rosette on absorbent paper to drain. Be sure to wipe iron and reheat each time before dipping into batter. Makes 45 rosettes. When cooled, sprinkle with powdered sugar.

Tips for Rosettes

- If they do not come off the iron, they are not done enough to do so.
- If blisters form, eggs have been beaten too much.
- If they are not crisp, they have been fried too slowly.
- If rosette falls into oil, you do not have enough flour in the batter.

Fattigmann

6 egg yolks
3 egg whites
6 tablespoons sugar
6 tablespoons cream

2 tablespoons melted butter
6 cardamom seeds
Flour
Fat for frying

Beat egg yolks and whites together until thick and lemon colored. Add sugar and continue beating. Add cream and beat again; blend in butter. Crush cardamom seeds to powder and add with enough flour to make a dough firm enough to roll. Roll thin as paper. Cut into diamond shapes about 5 x 2-1/2 inches. Deep-fry in hot fat 2 to 3 minutes or until golden brown. Drain on absorbent paper and sprinkle with powdered sugar.

Hjortetakk

4 eggs, beaten
1 cup sugar
3/4 cup melted butter
Grated peel of 1 orange and 1 lemon

1 teaspoon baking powder
4 cups flour
4 ounces brandy

Mix all the ingredients the day before to make dough. Refrigerate overnight. Roll small pieces of dough by hand into strips a bit thicker than a pencil and 5 inches long. Overlap the ends of each and fry in deep fat, as you would doughnuts, until browned.

Wafer Cones or Crumb Cake
Krumkake

3 eggs, well-beaten
1/2 cup sugar
1/2 cup butter, melted
1/4 teaspoon salt

1/2 teaspoon almond extract
1/2 teaspoon lemon extract
1/2 cup flour

Mix eggs, sugar, butter, salt, and flavorings. Beat well. Stir in flour. Heat Krumkake iron on medium heat. Pour a teaspoon of batter on iron. Bake 1 minute; turn iron over and bake until lightly browned. Remove from iron and quickly roll onto a cone-shaped form. Cool and store in an air-tight container.

Raspberry Cake
Bringebærkake

Cake
1-1/2 cups flour
1/2 cup sugar
1 teaspoon baking powder
1/2 cup butter
1 egg
1/2 cup raspberry jam, divided

Filling
1/2 cup butter

2/3 cup sugar
1/2 teaspoon almond extract
2 eggs
1 cup finely ground blanched almonds
    (ground like coarse meal)

Frosting
1/2 cup powdered sugar
2 teaspoons lemon juice

Cake: Blend flour, sugar, and baking powder. Add butter and mix, working with pastry blender or fingers. Add egg and blend with fork until flour is moistened. Press dough evenly on bottom of a greased 9 x 1-1/2-inch springform pan. Spread 1/4 cup raspberry jam over dough. Cover and chill while making filling.

Filling: Cream butter and sugar. Add extract. Add eggs one at a time, beating well; mix in ground almonds. Spoon filling on top of jam. Bake at 350° for 50 minutes. Cool in a pan and remove cake carefully. Spread remaining 1/4 cup jam over top.

Frosting: Combine frosting ingredients and drizzle on top of jam. Can be made ahead and frozen.

Wedding Cake
Kransekake

Although this recipe seems simple, try to bake a few practice rings before you do the real thing. These portions are for 18 concentric ring mold pans (found at Scandinavian specialty shops).

1 pound almond paste

1 pound powdered sugar, sifted

2 egg whites, unbeaten

1/4 cup powdered sugar for kneading

In large bowl, mix almond paste and powdered sugar. Add egg whites. Mix well. Place bowl in hot water and knead dough until lukewarm. Turn out on board sprinkled with 1/4 cup powdered sugar. Let rest 10 minutes. Knead 2 to 3 minutes. Press dough through cookie press into greased ring forms. Bake at 300° for 20 minutes.

Do not remove rings from forms until thoroughly cooled. Frost each ring and place on top of one another in a conical shape to form a tree with a hollow center.

1-1/2 cups powdered sugar, sifted   1 teaspoon vinegar
1 egg white, beaten

Frosting: Blend powdered sugar, egg white, and vinegar. Drizzle over cake rings as you stack. Cake freezes well. You can stack ring sections for easier storage and use more frosting for final assembly. **Note (if not using concentric baking pans):** With lightly floured hands, roll small amounts of dough into a 1/2-inch-thick strip, long enough to form width of base. Make each shorter. Dip ends into egg white and join. Place rings on lightly floured baking sheets.

Almond Cake
Fyrstekake

1-1/2 cups flour
1 teaspoon baking powder
1/2 cup sugar
1/2 cup plus 1 tablespoon butter
1 egg or 2 egg yolks

Filling
1 cup ground almonds
1 cup powdered sugar
2 egg whites, slightly beaten

Mix dry ingredients in mixing bowl. Blend in butter with a pastry blender or with fingertips until mixture resembles coarse flour. Beat in egg yolks. Chill. **Prepare filling:** Grind almonds once, then grind a second time with powdered sugar. Blend thoroughly with beaten egg whites until mixture is firm and smooth. Chill.

Press 2/3 of the chilled dough into a 6-inch round ungreased cake pan, covering sides and bottom. Spread almond mixture evenly over dough. Roll remainder of dough to 1/8 inch thickness and cut into 8 strips, 1/2 inch wide. Lay 4 strips parallel to each other across the top of the filling. Arrange remaining 4 strips at right angles, weaving to form a lattice pattern. Cut another 1/2-inch-wide strip and press around edge of cake. Bake at 375° for 25 to 30 minutes, or until golden brown.

Note: If you prefer blanched almonds, scald them; unblanched give better flavor. Cool cake on rack a few minutes before carefully loosening sides and removing from pan. Cut into wedges.

Almond Apple Cake
Mandel-Eplekake

2 cups apple slices (fresh or canned)

3 eggs

1/2 cup sugar

2/3 cup ground blanched almonds

If fresh apples are used, slice and boil with 1/4 cup water and additional 1/2 cup sugar 5 minutes. Drain and spread evenly in buttered baking dish. Beat eggs and sugar until whites are fluffy. Fold in almonds. Pour egg mixture over apples. Bake at 350° for 30 to 40 minutes. Serve cold with cream or vanilla sauce. Serves 6.

King Haakon Cake
Kong Haakon Kake

1 cup shortening
1-1/2 cups sugar
3 eggs, beaten
1 cup sour milk
2 tablespoons molasses
1 cup chopped dates
3 cups flour

1 teaspoon nutmeg
1 teaspoon salt
1 teaspoon baking soda
1 teaspoon baking powder
1 teaspoon cinnamon
1 cup chopped nuts

Cream shortening, sugar, and eggs. Stir in sour milk, molasses, and dates. Mix dry ingredients; add to creamed mixture. Pour into greased and floured 9 x 13-inch pan. Bake at 350° for 40 to 45 minutes.

Chocolate Cake
Sjokoladekake

3 egg whites
1-3/4 cups sugar, divided
1/2 cup shortening
1/4 teaspoon salt
1 teaspoon vanilla
1/2 cup cocoa

1/3 cup hot water
1 cup cold water
2-1/2 cups sifted flour
1-1/3 teaspoons baking soda
1/4 cup warm water

Beat egg whites and 3/4 cup sugar until fluffy. Set aside. Cream shortening, salt, 1 cup sugar, and vanilla. Set aside. Make cocoa/hot water paste; add to cream mixture; lightly blend. Add cold water and flour alternately to cream mixture. Fold in egg white mixture. Add soda dissolved in warm water; fold with wire whisk. Pour into greased 9 x 13-inch pan. Bake 35 to 40 minutes at 350°.

Mock Whipped Cream Frosting

1 egg
1 cup milk
1/2 cup sugar
2 tablespoons cornstarch
1/4 teaspoon salt

1 teaspoon vanilla
1/2 cup shortening
2 tablespoons butter
5 heaping tablespoons powdered sugar

In a double boiler, beat the egg, milk, sugar, cornstarch, and salt. Cook over water until thick. Add vanilla and cool. Cover until set but not hard. Beat together shortening, butter, and powdered sugar. Add to cooked egg mixture and beat until smooth. Good on chocolate cake.

Cloudberry Cream Pie
Multekrem Pai

Pastry

1/3 cup butter or margarine

2-1/2 tablespoons sugar

1/3 teaspoon salt

1 egg yolk

1/3 cup finely chopped almonds

1 cup flour

Filling

2 cups cloudberries, fresh or frozen

2 egg whites

1 cup sugar

1 tablespoon lemon juice

1/4 teaspoon vanilla

1/4 teaspoon almond extract

1/4 teaspoon salt

1 cup whipping cream

Pastry: Preheat oven to 400°. Grease 10-inch pie pan. Cream butter, sugar, and salt; add egg yolk and beat well. Stir in almonds and flour. Press into pan and bake 12 minutes, until lightly browned. Let cool.

Filling: Mix all filling ingredients except cream and heat until mixture thickens, 15 minutes. Cool. Whip cream and fold into cooled cloudberry mixture. Spoon into pastry and freeze at least 8 hours. Serves 12.

Caramel Pudding
Karamellpudding

2 cups and 2 tablespoons sugar, divided
3 tablespoons boiling water
3 egg yolks
1 cup milk

1 teaspoon vanilla
1/2 cup heavy cream, whipped
Chopped walnuts (optional)
3 cups puréed fruit (applesauce or berries)

Melt 2 cups sugar on low heat in heavy saucepan; stir until golden brown. Add boiling water slowly to melted sugar; blend well. In top of double boiler, combine egg yolks and remaining sugar, milk, and vanilla. Beat with wire whisk until foamy; cook until hot. Add sugar (cooled to "soft ball") to custard. Beat until smooth. Remove from heat; beat until cool. Fold whipped cream into cooled custard. Sprinkle with nuts. Chill and serve over fruit.

Caramel Ice
Karamell-is

2/3 cup sugar
1/4 cup strong boiled coffee

2/3 cup coarsely ground scalded
almonds
1 quart whipped cream

Stir sugar in heavy skillet over low heat until browned. Add coffee and almonds; stir until blended. Cool and fold into whipped cream. Chill thoroughly or freeze. Makes 6 servings.

Macaroni Pudding

1/2 pound uncooked macaroni
1-1/2 quarts milk
1 tablespoon sugar

1 tablespoon butter
4 egg yolks
4 egg whites, stiffly beaten

Cook macaroni in milk until tender. Remove from heat; add sugar and butter; mix thoroughly and let cool. Stir in egg yolks, one at a time; fold in stiffly beaten egg whites. Spoon into a greased and floured mold placed in a pan of boiling water. Bake at 300° for 1 hour. Let cool slightly before removing from mold. Unmold on a platter and serve with choice of sauce.

Bread Pudding
Brødpudding

4 cups stale, cubed bread
2 eggs or 4 egg yolks
2 cups milk

1/2 cup sugar
1 teaspoon nutmeg
Raisins (optional)

Spread bread cubes in a lightly greased baking dish. Beat eggs, milk, sugar, and nutmeg. Pour over bread and let stand 1 hour. Add raisins, if desired. Bake 30 minutes at 350°. Serve with cream, jelly, or pudding sauce.

Variations:

Fruit and nuts—Add 1 cup chopped dates, raisins, or figs; 1/2 cup nut meats.
Butterscotch—Instead of white sugar, use brown sugar and heat it with butter.

Dravle

2 quarts milk
2 eggs
1 quart buttermilk

1-1/2 cups sugar
1-1/2 cups raisins

Heat milk until it boils. Beat eggs into buttermilk. Add to hot milk slowly, to form cheese curds and whey. When cheese settles, reduce heat and simmer 15 to 20 minutes. Add sugar and raisins. Increase heat and cook 1/2 hour or longer. Thicken with cornstarch mixed with cream, if necessary.

Rømmegrøt

1 quart cream (not too fresh)   3/4 quart milk
1 cup flour (more if needed)   Sugar and salt to taste

Stirring constantly, bring cream to a full boil and boil until foam is gone. Add flour gradually to make a thick mush. Stir until butter appears. Remove butter and reserve. Bring milk to a boil. Add hot milk gradually to mush, stirring constantly. Simmer 10 to 20 minutes, stirring frequently until mixture thickens. Add sugar and salt to taste.

Serving suggestions: Top with reserved butter; serve with syrup or honey; garnish with cinnamon and sugar.

Lemon Custard
Sitronkrem

2 tablespoons butter
1 cup sugar
3 eggs, separated
4 tablespoons flour

Dash of salt
5 tablespoons lemon juice
Rind of 1 lemon, grated
1-1/2 cups milk

Cream butter, sugar, and egg yolks. Add flour, salt, lemon juice, and rind, then milk. Beat egg whites to stiff peaks. Fold into mixture. Spoon into greased custard cups. Place in pan of water and bake 45 minutes at 350°. Each cup will contain custard at the bottom and sponge cake at the top. Serves 8.

Rice Pudding
Risengryn Pudding

4 eggs, slightly beaten
1/2 cup sugar
Dash of salt
1 teaspoon vanilla

4 cups milk, scalded
3/4 cup uncooked rice
1 to 1-1/2 cups raisins (optional)

Mix eggs, sugar, salt, and vanilla. Add scalded milk. Add rice and raisins, if desired. Pour into a flat baking dish. Set in another pan of water and bake at 350° for 20 minutes. Stir and bake another 25 minutes.

Apple Dumplings with Cinnamon Sauce
Epler i Slåbrok med Kanel Saus

1-1/4 cups sifted flour
3/4 teaspoon salt
3/4 cup shortening
7 to 8 tablespoons ice water
6 tart apples, cored and pared
1-1/2 teaspoons cinnamon
1/2 cup sugar

1 tablespoon butter

Sauce
1 cup sugar
1/4 teaspoon cinnamon
4 tablespoons butter
2 cups water

Sift flour and salt together. Cut in shortening to a fine "meal" with some pea-sized particles. Sprinkle ice water over mixture and blend with fork. Roll out 1/8 inch thick on lightly floured board. (Divide dough for easier handling.)

Cut into six 7-inch squares. Place each apple on a square of pastry. Fill each center with cinnamon and sugar. Dot with butter. Moisten points of pastry with water. Bring opposite points up over apples and seal well. Place 2 inches apart in baking pan and chill thoroughly.

To prepare sauce: Mix all sauce ingredients in a saucepan. Boil 3 minutes. Pour hot sauce over chilled dumplings and bake 5 to 7 minutes at 500°. Serve dumplings with hot syrup and cream, if desired.

Sauces

Tips for Making Sauces

1. Never use high heat.

2. Remove sauces-in-progress from heat before stirring in fresh ingredients.

3. If additions to hot sauce are cold, adjust them by mixing in a separate container with small amount of the hot liquid before adding to the cooking pot. (This is especially important for egg- or cream-based sauces.)

Onion Sauce

Løksaus

This goes well with fried fish.

2 medium-sized onions, finely chopped
3 tablespoons butter or margarine
2 tablespoons flour
1/2 teaspoon salt
1/4 teaspoon black pepper
1/2 teaspoon sugar
1-1/2 cups milk
2 tablespoons chopped green pepper
 (optional)

Sauté onions in butter over medium heat until tender. Remove onions from skillet. Stir flour, salt, pepper, and sugar in remaining butter. Continue stirring over low heat. Gradually add milk. Cook and stir until sauce thickens. Stir in onions; cook until blended. Stir in green pepper, if desired.

Egg Sauce

Eggesaus

This recipe is very good with poached or baked cod.

1/4 pound butter
1/4 cup hot stock
2 hard-cooked eggs, finely chopped
1 tablespoon finely chopped parsley

1 medium-sized tomato, peeled,
   seeded, and chopped
1 tablespoon finely chopped chives
Salt and pepper to taste

Melt butter in a saucepan. Remove from heat and beat in hot stock. Stir in eggs, parsley, tomato, and chives. Salt and pepper to taste. Reheat to almost boiling, but do not cook. Serve immediately.

Horseradish Sauce

Pepperrot Saus

4 tablespoons grated horseradish (or prepared horseradish)

1 pint sour cream

1 teaspoon salt

1/8 teaspoon white pepper

2 tablespoons finely chopped onion

1 teaspoon vinegar

3 tablespoons finely chopped dill

Drain liquid from horseradish. Combine remaining ingredients. Mix until smooth. Makes 2 cups of sauce.

Shrimp Sauce
Rekesaus

3 tablespoons butter, divided
2 tablespoons flour
1 cup boiling water
Salt to taste

Paprika to taste
Juice of 1/2 lemon
1 egg yolk
1 cup or 1 (8-ounce) can shrimp

Melt (don't brown) 2 tablespoons butter. Blend in flour; gradually add boiling water, stirring until the mixture thickens and is smooth. Add salt, paprika, and lemon juice. Remove from heat; add slightly beaten egg yolk and shrimp, cleaned and broken into small pieces. Add remaining butter in bits just before serving. (You can use lobster meat for lobster sauce. If using lobster, omit egg yolk.)

Curry Sauce

Karrisaus

2 tablespoons butter
2 tablespoons flour
2 teaspoons curry powder
1/4 teaspoon salt

Paprika to taste
1 cup milk
Onion juice to taste

Melt the butter; blend in the flour mixed with curry powder, salt, and paprika. Add milk gradually, stirring until the sauce boils. Boil several minutes, stirring constantly. Add onion juice to taste.

Mock Hollandaise Sauce
Falsk Hollandais Saus

2 egg yolks (slightly beaten)
1/4 cup cream
1/2 teaspoon salt

1/8 teaspoon nutmeg
1/2 lemon
2 tablespoons butter

Beat the yolks and cream together with a fork. Add remaining ingredients, except butter, and cook in double boiler until thick, stirring constantly. Add butter slowly. Serve immediately.

Caper Sauce
Kaperssaus

3 tablespoons butter, divided
1 heaping tablespoon flour
1 cup boiling water or fish stock

Salt and pepper to taste
1/2 teaspoon lemon juice
2 tablespoons drained capers

Melt 2 tablespoons butter. Blend in flour. Add boiling water gradually. Stir until very smooth and cook until thick. Add the seasonings, lemon juice, and capers. Add 1 tablespoon butter in small pieces. Serve immediately.

Anchovy Sauce

Ansjossaus

1/2 teaspoon chopped onion
3 tablespoons butter
3 tablespoons flour
1 cup soup stock

1/3 teaspoon pepper
2 anchovies or prepared paste
1 teaspoon lemon juice
Salt to taste

Brown the onion in the butter. Remove onion. Brown the butter. Add flour and brown with butter. Add stock, stirring until smooth. Season with pepper and boil for 2 minutes, stirring constantly. Add anchovies, cleaned and chopped fine, or anchovy paste to taste. Stir in the lemon juice. Add salt if necessary.

Tomato Butter

Tomatsmør

8 tablespoons unsalted butter
2 tablespoons tomato paste

1/2 teaspoon salt
1/4 teaspoon sugar

Beat the butter until light and fluffy. Beat in tomato paste, salt, and sugar. Chill. Serve with hot grilled or fried fish.

Cucumber Sauce

Agurksaus

This is very good on cold, boiled fish.

1 cucumber
1/2 cup heavy cream (sweet or slightly
    sour)

1/2 teaspoon salt
Cayenne to taste
2 tablespoons vinegar

Pare, chop, and drain the cucumber. Chill all ingredients thoroughly in the refrigerator. Whip the cream and mix well with other ingredients. Serve immediately.

Whipped Cream Sauce

Fløtesaus

1 egg, separated
2 tablespoons powdered sugar

1/2 teaspoon vanilla
1/2 cup cream

Beat egg yolk; add powdered sugar and vanilla. Whip cream until stiff. Whip egg white until stiff but not dry. Fold cream into yolk mixture, then add beaten egg white. Fold until blended, but do not stir after peaks are formed.

Rum Egg Sauce

| 5 egg yolks | 5 tablespoons sugar |
| 2 egg whites | 1 tablespoon rum (or brandy) |

Whip egg yolks and whites together. Add sugar and beat until mixture has a custard-like consistency. Beat in rum or brandy. Serve with or over fresh fruits.

Table of Contents

Notes

Notes